Published by Barbour Books, an imprint of Barbour Publishing, Inc.,
P.O. Box 719, Uhrichsville, Ohio 44683
www.barbourbooks.com

 Member of the
Evangelical Christian
Publishers Association

Printed in China.

May God Bless Your Special Day

ELLYN SANNA
WITH VIOLA RUELKE GOMMER

DayMaker
GREETING BOOKS

I give thanks for your life today.
You make my life special just by being you.
May God bless you
today,
in the year to come,
and always.

On your special day, may God bless you. . .

with an ageless and enduring youthful spirit.
May He help you to see the unique gifts
you give back to life.
May He unfold for you
a year's worth of moment-by-moment blessings,
and may His grace shine not only on today. . .
but on all your dreams
for tomorrow as well.

Happy birthday!

The LORD bless you and keep you;
the LORD make his face shine upon you
and be gracious to you;
the LORD turn his face toward you
and give you peace.

NUMBERS 6:24–26 NIV

1

Forever Young

Don't worry about growing older.
Your attitude toward life and all it offers
seems to make your spirit younger with each year.

*There is no duty we so much underrate
as the duty of being happy.
By being happy we sow
anonymous benefits upon the world.*

ROBERT LOUIS STEVENSON

It's not the years that make us old. Instead, we get old
when responsibilities loom larger than joys,
when we lose our sense of humor,
when we forget how to play.
We're too busy for such foolishness. . .and our hearts
begin to wrinkle, our spiritual shoulders stoop, and everywhere we look we see only shades of gray.

Don't listen to what the world says about aging. Refuse to grow old.

See the delight life still has to offer.

Take time to laugh, to play,

to rejoice in all God has given us.

A child throwing coins into a fountain doesn't care if she's wasting money; she only knows she's having fun, and by doing so she spreads her joy. Be the same with life's pleasures: Don't worry about wasting time; instead, make room in your life for delight, and your joy will spread to others.

Time is the coin of your life.
It is the only coin you have,
and only you can determine how it will be spent.
Be careful lest you let other people spend it for you.

CARL SANDBURG

What Made You Happy When You Were Young?

Here is a list of the pleasures from my childhood:

_____

_____

_____

_____

_____

_____

_____

_____

_____

_____

_____

_____

_____

I am not too old to enjoy these pleasures again. This year I will take time to. . .

_____

_____

_____

_____

_____

_____

_____

_____

_____

May these simple pleasures help you be
more aware of that invisible world—
the kingdom of heaven—
in which we live.

The glory of the young is their strength;
the gray hair of experience is the splendor of the old.

PROVERBS 20:29 NLT

• • •

Each stage of your life
has its own special gifts and blessings.
May you never be too old to
take pleasure in all that God has made.

2
Your Gift to Life

Every good and perfect gift is from above.

JAMES 1:17 NIV

You have a very special place in my heart.
We have shared together the blessings of God.

PHILIPPIANS 1:7 NLT

• • •

Not only have we shared God's blessings. . .
He has also used you to be a blessing in my life.
I am so grateful for the many gifts
of time and love you've given me.
You make my life brighter with all you do.

We must use time creatively,
and forever realize that the time is
always right to do right.

MARTIN LUTHER KING, JR.

• • •

The purpose of our lives is
to give birth to the best which is within us.

MARIANNE WILLIAMSON

You are a birthday gift God has given to the world.
No one else could ever take your place,
for you are unique, one-of-a-kind.
No one else can demonstrate God's grace quite like you.
So celebrate your life!
Praise God for all His blessings.

• • •

There is only one of you in the world, just one,
and if that is not fulfilled then something has been lost.

MARTHA GRAHAM

Happiness is like perfume;
you can't pour it on someone else
without getting a few drops on yourself.

JAMES VAN DER ZEE

• • •

You bring joy to my heart.
You bring joy to God's heart.
And may your birthday be blessed with joy.
May the sweet perfume of joy fill your entire life.

He who pursues righteousness and love
finds life, prosperity, and honor.

PROVERBS 21:21 NIV

Your life is a signature of God's grace.

18

A Birthday Gift to the World

This year I will give a birthday gift back to God and the world around me by. . .

_____

_____

_____

_____

_____

_____

_____

_____

_____

_____

May your life be made richer by giving.

Life's most persistent and urgent question is,
What are you doing for others?

MARTIN LUTHER KING, JR.

• • •

Happy birthday to someone who
takes this question seriously!
All of us who know you appreciate all you do.

3

Moment–by–Moment Blessings

"God is love," says 1 John 4:16. In the year ahead,
may you encounter His love everywhere you turn.

The secret of health for mind and body
is not to mourn for the past,
not to worry about the future,
not to anticipate troubles,
but to live in the present moment
wisely and earnestly.

SIDDHARTHA GAUTAMA, 500 B.C.

Some people only exist.
They go through their days with their eyes on the ground,
plodding along as though life were an endurance test.
My prayer is that you will look up this year.
Dare to *live* rather than merely exist.
Don't miss the small joys and tiny blessings
God has showered on your life.

• • •

May you live all the days of your life.

JONATHAN SWIFT

Handmade Gifts

The Lord will fill your year with good things
made by His hands
just for you.

• • •

The well of Providence is deep.
It's the buckets we bring to it that are small.

MARY WEBB

Sometimes we're so focused on the big things—finances, health, our loved ones' well-being—that we forget to notice the many small blessings God showers on our lives. Each new sunrise, each good meal, each warm bath or good night's sleep, all send us love messages from our Father.

This year, take time for the small, moment-by-moment blessings God wants you to enjoy.

*Celebrate this new year of life
by giving yourself a gift of...*

A phone call to a special friend.
Lunch at a favorite restaurant with someone dear.
A book you've been wanting to read.
Time alone to savor something special.
A cup of tea or coffee or a tall, cool drink.
A walk through nature.

Treat yourself to some small gift each day this year. May each day that comes be a brand-new present to be unwrapped with joy.

A Birthday Pledge

In this new year of my life, I will take time for small pleasures like these:

_____

_____

_____

_____

_____

_____

_____

_____

_____

_____

_____

Happy birthday to me!

*If you can have just a little fun today,
it's a sign that maybe the future
will hold even more fun for you.
Fun isn't just fun—it's hope.*

LINDA RICHMAN

• • •

The real joy of life is in its play.
Play is anything we do for the joy and love of doing it,
apart from any profit, compulsion, or sense of duty.
It is the real living of life.

WALTER RAUSCHENBUSCH

4
Dreams for Tomorrow

Nothing happens unless first a dream.

CARL SANDBURG

Welcome this new year of your life with open arms.
The year will bring change;
face these changes with courage, joy, and dreams.
Seek new attitudes, new tasks, new treasures.
Let yesterday's pleasures go, like a child's worn-out toys.
God has new gifts to give you.
Hold out your hands.
Don't be afraid to open His packages of blessings.

There are years that ask questions
and years that answer.

ZORA NEALE HURSTON

• • •

Whether the year that lies ahead is one of answers
or of questions
or a little of both,
I pray that God's hand will touch you
through all the answers
and all the questions
life brings your way.
Don't be afraid to dream,
don't be afraid to ask.
Trust God to supply the answers in His good time.

Ask and it will be given to you;
seek and you will find;
knock and the door will be opened to you.
For everyone who asks receives;
he who seeks finds;
and to him who knocks, the door will be opened.

LUKE 11:9–10 NIV

Expect to have hope rekindled.
Expect your prayers to be answered in wondrous ways.
The dry seasons in life do not last.
The spring rains will come again.

SARAH BAN BREATHNACH

I pray each day of your new year
will nourish your spirit in new ways.
May you taste the goodness of God.
I pray each day will bring you
peace of mind and a joyful heart.
May you know God's love.

• • •

Where there is great love there are always miracles.

WILLA CATHER

In one hand I have a dream,
and in the other I have an obstacle.
Tell me, which one grabs your attention?

HENRY PARKS

• • •

The dream is the truth.

ZORA NEALE HURSTON

• • •

A dream is the bearer of a new possibility,
the enlarged horizon,
the great hope.

HOWARD THURMAN

*It takes great love and courage to
excavate buried dreams. . . .*

SARAH BAN BREATHNACH

Sometimes as we grow older, we let go of our dreams. They don't seem practical anymore; we don't have time for them in our busy schedules; and so those dreams that once seemed so bright and possible disappear beneath the weight of bills and household chores and other grown-up responsibilities.

But somewhere, deeply buried in your heart, those dreams still live. Dare to dig them up. Be brave enough to dream again.

Who knows what God will do?

Birthday Blessings

May God grant you. . .

B alance for a busy life.

i ndividuality and the confidence to be yourself.

r enewal of your spirit.

t hankfulness of heart.

h onor for yourself as God's special child.

d elight in each new day.

a chievement of your goals.

"y es" as your answer to God's will for your life.

Without dreams, human beings would accomplish very little. Dreams give us glimpses of a better world. Dreams inspire us to strive for something better. They push us out of our ruts. They give us wings to fly.

Flying is frightening of course. We never know when we might fall.

This new year, dare to fly, despite the risk. Trust the Spirit's wind beneath your wings.

Birthday Dreams

These are my dreams for the coming year:

_____

_____

_____

_____

_____

_____

_____

_____

_____

_____

*I place these dreams into God's hands.
I will trust Him to unfold
the future according to His plan.*

May this new year of your life
bring your dreams to reality.

• • •

Reach high, for stars lie hidden in your soul.
Dream deep, for every dream precedes the goal.

PAMELA VAULL STARR

• • •

*And may God bless
your special day!*